The Best Col........

of Filipino Recipes

Philippine's Cookbook of Authentic Dishes

BY: Valeria Ray

License Notes

Copyright © 2019 Valeria Ray All Rights Reserved

All rights to the content of this book are reserved by the Author without exception unless permission is given stating otherwise.

The Author have no claims as to the authenticity of the content and the Reader bears all responsibility and risk when following the content. The Author is not liable for any reparations, damages, accidents, injuries or other incidents occurring from the Reader following all or part of this publication.

A Special Reward for Purchasing My Book!

Thank you, cherished reader, for purchasing my book and taking the time to read it. As a special reward for your decision, I would like to offer a gift of free and discounted books directly to your inbox. All you need to do is fill in the box below with your email address and name to start getting amazing offers in the comfort of your own home. You will never miss an offer because a reminder will be sent to you. Never miss a deal and get great deals without having to leave the house! Subscribe now and start saving!

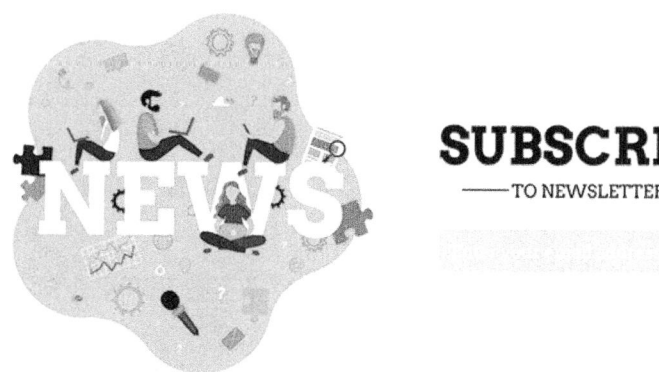

https://valeria-ray.gr8.com

Contents

Delicious Filipino Food Recipes

MMMMMMMMMMMMMMMMMMMMMMMMMMMMMMMM

(1) Tinolang Manok

This popular chicken soup recipe is a favorite for its refreshing taste. It is best cooked with papaya and chili leaves, which give the soup a unique character that is proudly its own. There are several versions of Tinola in different regions but the Tagalog version, the one prominent in the Northern part of the Philippines is the most common.

Yield: 8

Cooking Time: 45 minutes

List of Ingredients:

- 2 lbs. chicken, cut into serving pieces
- 2 pcs green papaya, cut into wedges
- ½ cup chili leaves
- 3 garlic cloves, minced
- 1 tablespoon ginger, cut into strips
- 1 pc onion, sliced
- 1 tablespoon fish Sauce
- 3 cups water
- 2 Tablespoons cooking oil

MMMMMMMMMMMMMMMMMMMMMMMMMMMMMMMM

Methods:

1. Heat oil in a pan over medium heat and sauté garlic, ginger, and onions until fragrant, about 5 minutes.
2. Add the chicken and continue stirring until meat changes in color.
3. Stir in the fish sauce and water, then, boil.
4. Cook in a simmer for half an hour until chicken is cooked through.
5. Add the papaya wedges and cook for about 5 minutes until soft.
6. Finally, stir in chili leaves, boil briskly for 2 minutes, and turn off heat.
7. Serve hot.

(2) Crispy Pata

Filipino food is packed with blood pressure bending recipes that are simply irresistible. This Crispy Pata or Crispy Pork Hock recipe is one of those. Naturally, this is done with tenderized whole pork hock that is deep-fried to a heavenly crispiness. But if the whole variety is not available, you may settle for pork hock slices, which are commonly available in grocery stores and supermarkets.

Yield: 6

Cooking Time: 55 minutes

List of Ingredients:

- 3 lbs. pork hock, rinsed
- 5 garlic cloves, crushed
- 1 bunch lemongrass, tied into a knot
- 1 tablespoon whole peppercorn
- 1 tablespoon salt
- 6 cups water
- 3 cups cooking oil

MMMMMMMMMMMMMMMMMMMMMMMMMMMMMMMMMM

Methods:

1. Combine the pork hock in a pressure cooker together with the water, garlic, lemongrass, peppercorn, and a half tablespoon of salt.
2. Pressure cook for 25 minutes or until the meat is tender.
3. After 25 minutes, remove the meat and pat it dry.
4. Rub the remaining salt onto the meat and let it sit for a few minutes.
5. Meanwhile, heat oil in a deep fryer or skillet over medium heat.
6. Fry the pork hock until golden brown and crispy. Drain on paper towels and serve.

(3) Dinuguan

One of the many interesting things to discover about Filipino cooks is how they manage to maximize the use of the ingredients available to them. Dinuguan or Pork Blood Stew is a product of that creativity. Instead of throwing away pork blood, they make use of it to create a somehow exotic delicacy that is surprisingly delicious!

Yield: 4

Cooking Time: 1 hour

List of Ingredients:

- 10 oz pork blood
- 1 lb. pork loin, cubed
- 1 tablespoon garlic, minced
- 1 pc onion, finely chopped
- 2 pcs long green pepper
- 1 cup vinegar
- 1 cup water
- 1 tablespoon vegetable oil
- Salt to taste

MMMMMMMMMMMMMMMMMMMMMMMMMMMMMMM

Methods:

1. Heat the oil in a pan over medium heat and sauté the garlic and onions.
2. Add the pork and stir occasionally for 5 minutes or until the meat is lightly browned.
3. Stir in the water and boil, then reduce the heat to low and simmer for 30 minutes or until pork is tender.
4. Gently add the vinegar and let it simmer on medium heat for 5 minutes.
5. Pour the pork blood in, stirring continuously for 10 minutes.
6. Add the green peppers and cook for 2 more minutes.
7. Serve.

(4) Bicol Express

Another proud Bicolano dish is this pork stew that has shrimp paste, coconut cream, and chilies. The flavors of those local ingredients give the dish some depth and an exciting play of flavors that you will love coming back to with a spoon. Interestingly, the beginning of this dish was traced back to a passenger train that service Manila to Bicol and vice versa. It was also where the name came from. This dish was sold widely in the passenger train by homemakers who want to make money for a living.

Yield: 5

Cooking Time: 40 minutes

List of Ingredients:

- 2 lbs. pork belly, sliced into bite-sized pieces
- 1 ½ cups coconut milk
- 1 tablespoon shrimp paste
- 3 garlic cloves, minced
- 1 pc onion, diced
- 1 pc tomato, diced
- 6 pcs red chilies, minced
- 2 Tablespoons oil, divided

MMMMMMMMMMMMMMMMMMMMMMMMMMMMMMMMMMM

Methods:

1. Heat a tablespoon of oil in a pan and sauté garlic, onions, and tomatoes until softened and fragrant.
2. Add the shrimp paste and pork until the meat is slightly browned.
3. Pour the coconut milk in and boil. Reduce the heat to low and simmer until the meat is tender, about 15 minutes.
4. Stir in the chilies and turn off the heat.

(5) Chicken and Pork Adobo

The classic Filipino stew has sprawled many different variations. For the meat kind, it is unclear which is more popular, Chicken Adobo or Pork Adobo. If you are curious about which tastes better, you can always put both ingredients in one recipe and make your Adobo doubly delightful.

Yield: 4

Cooking Time: 1 hour 20 minutes

List of Ingredients:

- 1 ½ lbs. chicken, cut into serving parts
- 1 ½ lbs. pork belly, cubed into 2-inch pieces
- 1 head garlic, minced
- 1 pc onion, thinly sliced
- 1 cup vinegar
- ½ cup soy sauce
- 1 tablespoon vegetable oil
- 1 cup water
- 2 pcs bay leaves
- Salt and pepper to taste

MMMMMMMMMMMMMMMMMMMMMMMMMMMMMMM

Methods:

1. Heat the oil in a skillet over medium heat.
2. Sauté the garlic until lightly brown and fragrant, about 3 minutes.
3. Add the onions and stir frequently for 2 minutes more.
4. Since the pork needs more time to get tender, put the pork cubes in first, stirring occasionally until evenly browned, about 10 minutes.
5. Stir in the chicken pieces and cook until they change in color.
6. Whisk in the vinegar and boil uncovered, making sure that you do not stir until after the mixture is boiling.
7. Next, stir in the soy sauce, bay leaves, and water. Bring to a boil.
8. Cover and simmer the mixture until the meats are tender and most of the liquid evaporated.
9. Adjust the seasoning with salt and some pepper.

(6) Fresh Lumpiang Ubod

The fresh spring rolls may be tedious to make since you will be in charge, from the wrapper to the filling, and finally the sauce. But all the efforts are worth it once you see your guests pleased with its delectable taste. This recipe is nothing like the Vietnamese spring rolls. It has its own, very unique character. For one, the wrapper is made of an egg batter, carefully made like a crepe. For another, the filling is characterized by strips of the heart of palm, which is derived from coconut trees that were taken down.

Yield: 6

Cooking Time: 1 hour

List of Ingredients:

For the Wrappers:

- 3 pcs eggs, beaten
- 1 cup cornstarch
- 1 ½ cups water
- 1 teaspoon sugar
- 1 teaspoon salt

For the Filling:

- 2 lbs. ubod, cut into matchsticks
- ¼ lb. pork belly, diced
- ½ lb. shrimp, peeled and coarsely chopped
- 2 garlic cloves, minced
- 1 pc onion, chopped
- 1 tablespoon fish sauce
- ½ cup water
- 1 tablespoon oil
- Salt and pepper to taste
- 8 pcs lettuce leaves, ends trimmed and leaves separated

For the Sauce:

- 1 cup unsalted peanuts, ground
- 2 Tablespoons peanut butter
- 1 head garlic, minced
- ¼ cup soy sauce
- ¾ cup brown sugar
- 3 Tablespoons cornstarch
- ½ teaspoons salt
- 2 ¾ cups water
- 1 tablespoon fried garlic bits
- 1 tablespoon ground peanuts

MMMMMMMMMMMMMMMMMMMMMMMMMMMMMMMMMM

Methods:

1. To make the wrappers, combine the cornstarch and water in a bowl, stirring until the cornstarch is dissolved.
2. Add the eggs, sugar, and salt and stir until the batter has a runny, thin consistency.

3. Pour about a quarter cup of batter onto a lightly greased nonstick pan. Cook for about a minute both sides. Slide into a plate and set aside.
4. For the filling, heat oil in a skillet over medium heat and sauté garlic and onions.
5. Add pork and shrimp, cook for 5 minutes.
6. Pour water and simmer to make the meat tender.
7. Then, add the ubod strips and cook for another 10 minutes.
8. Season with salt and pepper, then, transfer in a plate to cool, draining liquids.
9. For the sauce, add the soy sauce, 2 and ½ cups of water, brown sugar, and a bit of salt to the saucepan and boil over medium heat, stirring frequently to dissolve sugar.
10. Add the garlic and ground peanuts. Stir to blend.
11. Finally, dissolve cornstarch into the remaining water. Whisk into the sauce mixture and stir until thick.
12. To assemble, lay down a piece of a wrapper on your work surface, place a lettuce leaf on top, and scoop about ¼ cup of filling, then, roll.
13. Garnish spring roll with sauce and a sprinkle of fried garlic bits and ground peanuts.

(7) Bulalo

A widely popular beef dish all over the country, Bulalo is a hearty and rich Filipino beef soup made from shanks. The many hours it will take to wait for the meat to be ready are all worth it because you get a delicious meal that offers a warm embrace with every mouthful. It does not require a lot of ingredients; just a lot of patience.

In the past, before the pressure cooker was introduced to households, the local cooks would painstakingly wait for 3-4 hours until the meat was fork-tender and had that melt-in-your-mouth goodness. Thanks to technology, that amount of time is considerably reduced although no one would stop you from going the traditional way, especially if your kitchen is not equipped with a pressure cooker.

Yield: 4

Cooking Time: 1 hour 5 minutes

List of Ingredients:

- 2 ½ lbs. beef shanks slices
- 8 cups beef stock
- 1 pc sweet corn, sliced into 5 pieces
- 12 oz Napa cabbage, leaves separated
- 18 pcs green beans, trimmed
- 1 pc onion, cut into wedges
- 1 tablespoon whole peppercorn
- 3 Tablespoons fish sauce

MMMMMMMMMMMMMMMMMMMMMMMMMMMMMMMMMM

Methods:

1. Boil the stock, beef shanks, onions, peppercorns, and fish sauce in a pressure cooker.
2. Place the lid on and set the timer to 45 minutes.
3. When time's up, remove the lid. Add the sweet corn slices and cook until the corn is tender, or for about 15 minutes.
4. Stir in the green beans. Adjust the seasoning by adding more fish sauce according to your taste.
5. Arrange the Napa cabbage leaves in a serving bowl.
6. Empty the contents of the pressure cooker into a prepared bowl. Serve hot.

(8) Kinilaw na Tanigue

With its many islands and coastal regions, Ceviche is a favorite dish that the Filipinos found to do with their fresh catch. In this recipe, tanigue is used but other fish varieties like milkfish and others. In recipes like this, no heat is needed to cook the fish meat. Instead, it is soaked in acids and allow the calamansi juice to cook the meat.

Yield: 6

Cooking Time: 3 hrs 1 min

List of Ingredients:

- 2 lbs. tanigue fillet, cut into cubes
- 2 Tablespoons fresh ginger, minced
- 1 pc red onion, roughly chopped
- 8 pcs chilies, chopped
- Juice of 20 pcs calamansi
- ½ teaspoon sugar
- Salt and pepper to taste

MMMMMMMMMMMMMMMMMMMMMMMMMMMMMMMMMMMMM

Methods:

1. Combine all of the ingredients together in a bowl, except for the fish, until well-blended and the sugar is dissolved.
2. Pour the mixture onto fish and stir to blend. Adjust salt and pepper as needed.
3. Allow it to sit in the refrigerator to chill for at least 3 hours before serving.

(9) Lumpiang Shanghai

With its name bearing one of China's most popular cities, people thought that this dish originated from Shanghai. No such food exists in that city. It is true, however, that lumpia and the many varieties of it was of Chinese influence. They brought in the idea for spring rolls from the Fujian province to the rest of Southeast Asia. Philippines and Indonesia are the top countries that took the art of stuffing sheets of the wrapper with varying concoctions seriously.

Yield: 10

Cooking Time: 35 minutes

List of Ingredients:

- 30 pcs lumpia wrappers
- 1 lb. ground pork
- 1 cup shrimps, shelled and chopped
- ½ cup carrots, finely chopped
- ¼ cup onions, finely chopped
- 1 teaspoon sesame oil
- 3 Tablespoons soy sauce
- 2 pcs eggs, lightly beaten
- Salt and pepper, to taste
- 2 cups vegetable oil

MMMMMMMMMMMMMMMMMMMMMMMMMMMMMMMMMM

Methods:

1. Combine all of the ingredients in a bowl, stirring until blended.
2. Spoon the mixture on a piece of lumpia wrapper and roll it into a log. Repeat with the rest of the ingredients.
3. You can cut the rolls into two to make them easier to fry or fry them as is.
4. Heat the oil in a deep fryer or skillet.
5. Fry the spring rolls until brown, crispy, and cooked through. Serve.

(10) Leche Flan

The all-time Filipino favorite dessert is this egg custard steamed to perfection for a melts-in-your-mouth finish. Leche Flan can be eaten on its own or is used to make other dishes, such as Halo-Halo, extra delightful. This is commonly the dessert of choice during gatherings and parties.

Yield: 6

Cooking Time: 1 hour 30 minutes

List of Ingredients:

- 10 pcs egg yolks
- 1 can condensed milk
- 1 can evaporated milk
- 1 cup sugar
- 1 teaspoon vanilla extract

For the caramel:

- 1 cup sugar
- ¾ cup water

MMMMMMMMMMMMMMMMMMMMMMMMMMMMMMMM

Methods:

1. Prepare the caramel first by boiling sugar and water in a saucepan until nice and brown.
2. Meanwhile, mix together the egg yolks, milks, sugar, and vanilla extract until sugar is dissolved.
3. Pour the caramel onto molds before filling it in with the custard mixture.
4. Secure the molds with aluminum foil and rubber band.
5. Steam for 45 minutes to 1 hour.
6. Allow the Leche Flan to cool before transferring onto a serving plate.

(11) Sinangag

This Filipino fried rice is as versatile as all the other recipes in this cookbook. You can practically put anything you fancy in a stir-fry – from meats to vegetables to seasonings and spice. You have the liberty to choose what's in your pantry and what fits your fancy as well. Filipino cooking is very much like that. Homemakers dish out anything from among the available ingredients they can find, either in their ever-reliable pantry or, in some provinces, right in their very own backyard.

Yield: 4

Cooking Time: 25 minutes

List of Ingredients:

- 4 cups leftover rice, separated
- ¼ cup ham, cubed
- ¼ cup shrimp, shelled and chopped
- 6 garlic cloves, minced
- 1 tablespoon scallions, chopped
- 2 pcs eggs, cooked scrambled style and sliced
- 2 Tablespoons vegetable oil
- Salt and pepper to taste

MMMMMMMMMMMMMMMMMMMMMMMMMMMMMMMMMMMM

Methods:

1. Heat the oil in a wok over high.
2. Sauté the garlic to brown, then add the ham and shrimp. Season with a bit of salt and stir until blended.
3. Add the rice, stirring frequently until cooked through.
4. Stir in the sliced egg scramble and scallions.
5. Season with salt and pepper, mixing until well combined. Serve.

(12) Pork Menudo

This dish is both Chinese and Spanish in nature. The use of soy sauce together with tomato sauce is a very Filipino technique. It provides a balanced, rich flavor that is best eaten with steaming hot white rice. Menudo is a favorite everyday meal and is also a main player in most *fiestas* or parties and other types of gathering. It is not too complicated to prepare yet provides an amazing result each time.

Yield: 4

Cooking Time: 50 minutes

List of Ingredients:

- 1 lb. pork, cubed
- ½ lb. pork liver, cubed
- 5 pcs chorizo Bilbao, sliced
- 4 pcs potatoes, diced and fried
- 1 pc carrot, diced and fried
- 2 pc bell peppers, diced
- 1 cup chickpeas
- ¼ cup raisins
- 1 head garlic, minced
- 1 pc onion, diced
- 3 pcs tomatoes, diced
- 1 cup pork stock
- ½ teaspoons paprika
- 4 Tablespoons soy sauce
- 2 teaspoons fish sauce
- 3 Tablespoons vegetable oil
- 1 tablespoon annatto oil
- Salt and pepper to taste

MMMMMMMMMMMMMMMMMMMMMMMMMMMMMMMMMMM

Methods:

1. Heat the vegetable and annatto oil in a pan over medium heat and sauté garlic, onions, and tomatoes.
2. Add the pork, liver, and chorizo, stirring frequently for about 5 minutes.
3. Stir in the soy sauce, paprika, fish sauce, and stock.
4. Boil, then reduce heat to low and cook in a simmer until meats are tender, about 20 minutes.
5. Add the remaining ingredients, season with salt and pepper, and boil briskly for 5 more minutes before turning off heat.

(13) Pakbet

One of the most popular vegetable recipes in the Philippines is this Ilocano dish that features a number of locally abundant veggies, pork, and fermented shrimp sauce. It is signature dish up north, in the Ilocos region, but other provinces have since adapted the recipe and made it their own. Don't be surprised if you find versions with coconut milk in it or one that was cooked in a stir-fry instead of traditional boiling.

Yield: 4

Cooking Time: 35 minutes

List of Ingredients:

- 3 pcs string beans, trimmed, and cut into 2-inch pieces
- 2 cups squash, cut into chunks
- 1 pc eggplant, sliced
- 5 pcs okras, sliced diagonally
- 1 pc ampalaya, sliced
- ¼ lb. pork ribs, sliced
- 1 pc onion, sliced
- 1 pc tomato, diced
- 2 cups water
- ½ cup fermented shrimp sauce

MMMMMMMMMMMMMMMMMMMMMMMMMMMMMMMMM

Methods:

1. Heat the shrimp sauce in a pot. Add the pork slices and sauté until they change in color.
2. Add the water and boil. Reduce the heat and tenderize the meat at a simmer or for about 15 minutes.
3. Stir in all of the remaining ingredients and cook until tender.
4. Add more shrimp sauce according to your tastes.

(14) Palabok

The Philippines has several noodle recipes up its sleeves. Pancit Palabok is one of the most interesting with its rich shrimp gravy and a delightful set of toppings that make eating it an adventure on its own. The use of noodles in the recipe may associate it with a Chinese origin but it has been exclusively 'Filipino' from there and beyond. The toppings, which usually composed of flaked smoked fish, shrimps, hard-boiled eggs, crushed pork cracklings, sliced green onions, and crunchy garlic bits, make the dish extravagant and tasty.

Yield: 6

Cooking Time: 1 hour

List of Ingredients:

- 1 8oz package rice noodles, cooked according to package directions
- ½ lb. shrimp
- 1 cup pork cracklings, crushed
- ½ cup tinapa flakes, roasted
- ½ pound bacon, diced and cooked until crisp
- 4 pcs hard boiled eggs, peeled and quartered
- 1 head garlic, minced and fried
- ¼ cup green onions, chopped
- 1 tablespoon annatto powder
- 1 tablespoon bacon grease
- 1 tablespoon garlic oil
- 5 cups shrimp broth
- ¼ cup flour
- Salt and pepper to taste
- 6 pcs calamansi, halved

MMMMMMMMMMMMMMMMMMMMMMMMMMMMMMMMMMMM

Methods:

1. Mix together the shrimp broth, flour, annatto powder, bacon grease, and garlic oil in a saucepan over medium heat. Stir frequently until the solids dissolve.

2. Cook the sauce for 5 minutes until thickened. Season with salt and pepper.

3. Divide the cooked noodles onto 6 plates. Spoon the shrimp sauce and garnish with the toppings. Served with calamansi.

(15) Arroz Caldo

This rice soup, which brings warmth in every tasty bowl, is a good representation of how the local Filipino food has been influenced by other nations who tried to occupy it. The name *Arroz Caldo* is Spanish in nature, with a literal translation of 'hot rice.' On the other hand, the character of the dish is very similar to the Chinese version of the congee.

Yield: 8

Cooking Time: 35 minutes

List of Ingredients:

- 1 cup jasmine rice
- 2 lbs. chicken, cut into bite-size pieces
- 3 garlic cloves, minced
- 1 pc onion, chopped
- 3 Tablespoons ginger, sliced
- 8 cups chicken stock
- 2 Tablespoons vegetable oil
- 2 Tablespoons fish sauce
- ½ teaspoons freshly ground black pepper
- 4 pcs scallions, finely sliced

MMMMMMMMMMMMMMMMMMMMMMMMMMMMMMM

Methods:

1. Heat the oil in a pot over medium heat.
2. Sauté the garlic, ginger, and onions for about 5 minutes or until fragrant.
3. Add the chicken pieces and stir until they change in color.
4. Stir in the rice and stock, season with fish sauce and pepper, and boil.
5. Then, reduce the heat to low and continue cooking on a simmer for about 20 minutes, stirring occasionally.
6. Garnish with sliced scallions before serving.

(16) Beef Tapa

Beef Tapa is the main feature in a popular Filipino rice meal usually ordered for breakfast and every mealtime therein: Tapsilog. It is best enjoyed with a sunny side up egg and *Sinangag* (featured earlier). The secret to a truly delicious Tapa is making sure the meat is tender and well marinated. It is not too difficult to make but might take patience as you wait for the meat to absorb the flavors of the marinade.

Yield: 4

Cooking Time: 30 minutes

List of Ingredients:

- 1 lb. lean beef, thinly sliced into strips
- 1 head garlic, minced
- ½ cup fish sauce
- ¼ cup brown sugar
- 3 teaspoons salt
- 1 teaspoon ground pepper
- ½ cup cooking oil

MMMMMMMMMMMMMMMMMMMMMMMMMMMMMMMMMMMM

Methods:

1. Mix all of the ingredients in a bowl, except for oil. Turn the meat frequently to coat with the marinade.
2. Allow it to sit for an hour or overnight, stirring occasionally.
3. When the meat is ready, heat the oil in a pan over medium heat.
4. Fry the meat until browned, about 15 minutes, stirring frequently.
5. Serve with a plate of fried rice and sunny side up egg.

(17) Palitaw

Filipinos have discovered about a hundred and one ways to use sticky rice, especially in making rice cake delicacies of varying flavors and colors. *Palitaw* is one of the most interesting recipes. The name was derived from the fact that one will know when the sticky rice flour dumpling is cooked when it 'floats' into the surface. *Palitaw* literally translates 'to float.'

Yield: 4

Cooking Time: 35 minutes

List of Ingredients:

- 2 cups glutinous rice flour
- 1 cup water
- 2 Tablespoons sesame seeds, toasted
- ½ cup sugar
- 1 ½ cups grated coconut

MMMMMMMMMMMMMMMMMMMMMMMMMMMMMM

Methods:

1. Combine the glutinous rice flour and water in a bowl. Mix to form a dough.

2. Get a tablespoon of dough and form it into a ball, then press to make a tongue-shaped dumpling.

3. Boil about two quarts water in a pot. Cook the dumplings in batches, about 2 to 4 pieces each time. You do not want to overcrowd the pot to keep the dumplings separate.

4. Meanwhile, combine the sugar and sesame seeds in a bowl and place the coconut in a separate bowl. Set aside.

5. Wait until the dumplings surface to the top. Once cooked, roll the dumplings onto grated coconut, then in the sugar and sesame seeds mixture.

6. Arrange on a platter and serve.

(18) Papis

The main islands of the Philippines – Luzon, Visayas, and Mindanao – offer a lot of impressive recipes that are worth trying. Papis is Mindanao's pride. It features beef tendons and meat and a simple cooking technique. That said, you could not underestimate how delicious the result would be. You will definitely love it.

Yield: 4

Cooking Time: 35 minutes

List of Ingredients:

- 1 lb. beef tendons, cut into strips
- 1 lb. lean beef, sliced
- 1 14.5oz can pork and beans
- 2 pcs onions, chopped
- ½ cup water
- Salt and pepper to taste
- 2 Tablespoons vegetable oil

MMMMMMMMMMMMMMMMMMMMMMMMMMMMMMMMM

Methods:

1. Heat the oil in a pan over medium heat and sauté onions until fragrant, about 2 minutes.
2. Add the meat and brown, stirring frequently for 5 minutes.
3. Season the meat with salt and pepper, add water and cook for 15 minutes until tender and the liquids are absorbed.
4. Pour in the pork and beans and boil.
5. Reduce the heat to low and simmer for 10 minutes.
6. Serve hot.

(19) Tokneneng

The street food market in the Philippines is lively and Tokneneng is one of the usual treats. The orange-colored egg gets a lot of applause with its crunchy exterior and the tasty boiled interior. It's a great snack to prepare at home.

Yield: 4

Cooking Time: 25 minutes

List of Ingredients:

- 12 pcs hard-boiled eggs, peeled
- 2 cups vegetable oil
- 4 Tablespoons cornstarch
- 1 cup all-purpose flour
- ½ cup water
- Red and yellow food coloring
- Salt and pepper to taste

For the Sauce:

- ¼ cup rice vinegar
- 2 teaspoons soy sauce
- ¼ cup ketchup
- ¼ cup brown sugar

MMMMMMMMMMMMMMMMMMMMMMMMMMMMMMMMM

Methods:

1. To make the sauce, heat the ingredients in a saucepan over medium-low heat. Stir continuously for 5 minutes until the sugar dissolves. Transfer to a bowl and set aside.
2. Gently coat hard-boiled eggs in cornstarch. Set aside.
3. Combine the food coloring and water, stirring to blend.
4. In a bowl, mix together the flour, salt, and pepper.
5. Add the colored water. Mix until no lumps appear.
6. Preheat the oil in a deep fryer until the temperature reaches 375 °F.
7. Dip the cornstarch-coated eggs into the batter, turning a few times to coat.
8. Drop the eggs into the deep fryer, cooking in batches, for about 2 minutes or until the orange batter turns crispy.
9. Drain the fried eggs in paper towels, then, serve on a platter with the prepared sauce.

(20) Ginataang Kuhol

Another rich and flavorful dish that is worth trying is this recipe featuring apple snails cooked in coconut milk. This delicacy is a favorite all over the country and can even be considered an exotic dish. If you are overseas and snails in the shell are not available, you can always find the frozen kind, shelled and cleaned and ready to cook. By using the shelled kind, however, you will skip the thrill of sucking the meat out.

Yield: 4

Cooking Time: 45 minutes

List of Ingredients:

- 1 lb. apple snails (*kuhol*), shell removed
- 2 cups coconut milk
- 1 bunch fresh spinach, trimmed
- 6 pcs red chilies, roughly chopped
- 4 garlic cloves, minced
- 2 Tablespoons ginger, sliced
- 1 pc onion, sliced
- ¼ cup shrimp paste
- ¼ teaspoons ground black pepper
- 3 Tablespoons cooking oil

MMMMMMMMMMMMMMMMMMMMMMMMMMMMMMMM

Methods:

1. Heat the oil in a pan over medium heat and sauté garlic, ginger, and onions for about 2 minutes or until fragrant.

2. Put the apple snails and cook for 2 minutes, stirring occasionally.

3. Stir in the shrimp paste and chilies, then, pour in coconut milk and boil.

4. Reduce heat to low and continue cooking in a simmer for about half an hour.

5. Add the spinach, season with some pepper, and adjust heat to medium-high again. Cook for about five minutes.

(21) Sinigang

This sour soup dish is one of the many favorites in the Philippines. It is prominent in most regions, sprawling different variations each time. The most commonly used meat for this dish is pork, especially the bony parts, including ribs, neck bone, and tailbones. Other sinigang types may also feature chicken, beef, shrimp, fish, and other meats. The souring agent may also vary, according to preference and availability of the ingredients.

The most common is tamarind fruit but others also use ripe guava, green mango, wild mangosteen, kamias, tomatoes, and even tamarind blooms. In the Visayas region, where there is a scarce supply of tamarind, another fruit called *batwan* is used. There may be tamarind concentrates widely available in the market to keep up with the Filipinos' constant yearning of SInigang and to cut the process short but freshly squeezed tamarind fruit still provides the best taste.

Yield: 6

Cooking Time: 1 hour 10 minutes

List of Ingredients:

- 2 lbs. pork spare ribs, cut into serving pieces
- ½ lb. tamarind fruit, boiled and juice extracted
- 2 pcs taro, peeled and quartered
- 10 pcs string beans, trimmed and cut into 2-inch pieces
- 1 bunch spinach, trimmed
- 1 pc onion, sliced
- 2 pcs tomatoes, quartered
- 3 pieces long green chilies
- 2 liters of water
- 3 Tablespoons fish sauce

Methods:

1. Boil the water in a pot with the onions and tomatoes over medium heat. You may also boil tamarind fruits in this until they are soft.

2. Transfer the tamarind fruits in a bowl, then squeeze the juices out. Pass through a strainer and discard the solid pieces. Set aside.

3. Add the pork pieces and fish sauce. Cook in a simmer until the meat is tender, or for about 40 minutes.

4. Stir in the tamarind juice, taro, and chilies, mixing to blend.

5. After 5-10 minutes, add the string beans and cook for additional 5 minutes.

6. Finally, add the spinach. Add more fish sauce as needed, then turn off the heat.

7. Serve hot.

(22) Sisig

Sizzling sisig is a favorite treat among beer drinkers with its rich, spicy, salty, and utterly delicious taste. Other times, it is also served with hot, steamy rice for a delightful meal. Sisig is an original recipe from Pampanga province in Luzon. It is often cooked in a pan, then, transferred in a sizzling plate before cracking a fresh egg for that exciting finish.

Yield: 4

Cooking Time: 3 hours 20 minutes

List of Ingredients:

- ½ pork snout
- 1 pc pig ear
- 1 pc pork jowl
- ½ pork tongue
- 15 garlic cloves, minced
- 1 tablespoon ginger, chopped
- 4 pcs bird's eye chili peppers, chopped
- 1 pc white onion, diced
- 2 Tablespoons calamansi juice
- 1 ¼ cups soy sauce
- 2/3 cup coconut vinegar
- 3 Tablespoons salt
- 1 teaspoon whole peppercorns
- 1 ½ Tablespoons sugar
- 4 pcs eggs
- 1 tablespoon butter
- 1 teaspoon vegetable oil

MMMMMMMMMMMMMMMMMMMMMMMMMMMMMMMMMMM

Methods:

1. Place the pork pieces in a stockpot together with a cup of soy sauce, ½ cup vinegar, salt, peppercorns, sugar, and 10 garlic cloves. Mix to blend and then, boil.
2. Reduce heat to low and cook in a simmer for an hour and a half until meat is very tender.
3. Remove the pork from stock and set aside in the refrigerator to chill.
4. Char the meat pieces in a stovetop or charcoal, then put again in the fridge.
5. Dice charred meat and set aside.
6. Heat oil and butter in a pan over medium heat and sauté garlic and onions until fragrant.
7. Stir in the remaining ingredients except for egg and mix to blend.
8. Divide into four sizzling plates and crack an egg on top.
9. Serve hot.

(23) Kare-Kare

Kare-Kare or Oxtail and Vegetable Stew in Peanut Sauce is a traditional Filipino dish. It takes a good amount of time to cook and the process is quite complex but the result makes all the effort worth it. For the most part, oxtail is the meat of choice for the dish. Knowing Filipinos, who can provide different twists to favorite meals, you can also see Kare-Kare versions with beef loin, pork leg, tripe, and even seafood. Traditionally, Kare-Kare is cooked with close to a bland saltiness. That's because it is paired with shrimp paste to adjust and add even more flavors.

Yield: 6

Cooking Time: 3 hours 30 minutes

List of Ingredients:

- 3 lbs. oxtail, sliced into 2-inch pieces
- 1 pc banana flower bud, sliced into 2-inch pieces
- 3 pcs eggplants, halved and sliced into 2-inch pieces
- 15 pcs string beans, trimmed and cut into 2-inch pieces
- 1 bunch pechay or bok choy, trimmed and separated
- 3 garlic cloves, minced
- 1 pc onion, sliced
- ½ cup unsweetened peanut butter
- ¼ cup rice flour, toasted
- ¼ cup annato seeds, soaked in 1 cup water
- 6 cups water
- 2 Tablespoons vegetable oil
- Salt and pepper to taste
- ½ cup shrimp paste

MMMMMMMMMMMMMMMMMMMMMMMMMMMMMMMMMM

Methods:

1. Boil the oxtail in a pot of salted water on high. Reduce the heat to low and simmer for about 3 hours until tender. Remember to remove the scum after the first boil. Alternately, you may use a pressure cooker to shorten the process and make it 35-45 minutes instead of 3 hours. When the meat is tender, move it from the pot, pat dry, and set aside. Reserve the stock.

2. Heat the oil in a pan over medium heat. Brown oxtail on both sides. Remove from oil, then sauté the minced garlic and sliced onions until fragrant.

3. Put back browned oxtail and reserved stock together with annatto water, rice flour, salt, and pepper.

4. Put a cup of boiling stock onto peanut butter to dissolve, then, pour it onto the stew.

5. Add the vegetables, starting off with string beans. After two minutes, add the eggplant, then, banana flower bud, and finally, pechay. Cook for 8-10 minutes until the sauce thickens.

6. Serve with shrimp paste.

(24) Halo-Halo

This sweet Filipino dessert looks extravagant at first sight, with a number of ingredients that go into the cup together with finely shaved ice, sugar, and evaporated milk. This is widely sold in the streets and in restaurants, usually topped with ice cream, egg custard, and purple yam. It's a favorite delight, especially when the summer heat starts to strengthen.

Yield: 2

Cooking Time: 10 minutes

List of Ingredients:

- 2 Tablespoons saba banana slices, sweetened
- 2 Tablespoons sweet potato, diced and sweetened
- 2 Tablespoons red mung beans, boiled
- 1 tablespoon sugar palm seeds
- 2 Tablespoons tapioca pearls
- 2 Tablespoons macapuno strips, sweetened
- 1 tablespoon jackfruit strips, sweetened
- 1 tablespoon immature glutinous rice flakes, roasted and pounded
- 2 teaspoons sugar
- 2 cups ice, finely shaved
- ½ cup evaporated milk
- 1 tablespoon leche flan
- 1 tablespoon purple yam
- 2 scoops vanilla ice cream

Methods:

1. Separate all of the ingredients in two tall glasses, except for the milk, leche flan, purple yam, and vanilla ice cream.
2. Pour the milk on top of the ice, then garnish with leche flan, purple yam, and a scoop of vanilla ice cream each. Serve.

(25) Ampalaya Guisado

To appreciate bitter melon or bitter gourd, known locally as *ampalaya*, you have to develop an acquired taste. You will only appreciate it once you get used to it but believe it or not, Filipinos love this dish and prepare it too often. Some don't even need to do hacks in order to reduce the bitter taste and in fact, yearn for that flavor as it blends along with the other ingredients such as shrimp and pork.

Bitter gourd is among the many vegetables that are grown locally in many provinces all over the country.

Yield: 4

Cooking Time: 20 minutes

List of Ingredients:

- 1 pc ampalaya, cored and thinly sliced
- 10 pcs shrimps, shelled but tails intact
- 15 oz pork, sliced into small chunks
- 3 garlic cloves, minced
- 1 pc onion, chopped
- 1 pc tomato, chopped
- ½ teaspoons garlic powder
- 1 pc egg, beaten until smooth
- 3 Tablespoons cooking oil
- Salt and pepper to taste

MMMMMMMMMMMMMMMMMMMMMMMMMMMMMMMMM

Methods:

1. Rub the garlic powder, salt, and pepper onto shrimp. Let them sit for about five minutes.
2. Heat the oil in a wok over medium heat. Pan-fry the shrimp until they turn pink, about a minute each side. Put them in a bowl and set aside.
3. In the same wok, sauté the garlic, onions, and tomatoes for about 5 minutes.
4. Add the pork chunks and stir until a bit browned about 5 minutes.
5. Add the ampalaya and stir-fry for about 3 minutes.
6. Whisk in the beaten egg and cooked shrimp. Mix to blend.
7. Season with more salt and pepper to taste. Serve.

(26) Chicken Inasal

A popular recipe in the Visayas, specifically in Bacolod City, Chicken Inasal is simply marinated, grilled chicken. Unlike any other recipe of this kind, however, this offers the distinction of being the best and the most original out there and it is very *Pinoy*.

Yield: 4

Cooking Time: 1 hour 15 minutes

List of Ingredients:

- 4 pcs chicken leg
- 3 garlic cloves, crushed
- 1 teaspoon ginger, grated
- 3 Tablespoons calamansi juice
- 2 Tablespoons soy sauce
- 2 Tablespoons vinegar
- 1 tablespoon brown sugar
- 2 teaspoons salt

MMMMMMMMMMMMMMMMMMMMMMMMMMMMMMMMMM

Methods:

1. Combine all of the marinade ingredients in a bowl, stirring to dissolve the sugar and salt.
2. Place chicken onto the bowl, turning to coat with the marinade. Set aside in the refrigerator for 30 minutes or overnight.
3. Skewer chicken in a bamboo stick. Grill for 20 minutes, turning occasionally until meat is cooked through.

(27) Empanada

The Ilocos region features a lot of interesting dishes that are its own. This empanada recipe is one of their originals. It is a common sight in Vigan, Ilocos Sur, which, by the way, is an in-demand tourist attraction among foreign and local travelers alike. It's a favorite street food treat and is mostly eaten with a vinegar dipping sauce. This delicacy features another Vigan favorite, the famous longganisa, which is a must-buy for everyone.

Yield: 6

Cooking Time: 55 minutes

List of Ingredients:

For the Pastry Dough:

- 1 ½ cups all-purpose flour
- 1/3 cup butter, melted
- ½ cup annatto water
- 2 cups vegetable oil, divided

For the Filling:

- 6 pcs longganisa, separated
- 1 pc green papaya, shredded
- 6 pcs eggs
- 2 garlic cloves, finely chopped
- 1 pc onion, chopped
- Salt and pepper to taste

MMMMMMMMMMMMMMMMMMMMMMMMMMMMMMMMMM

Methods:

1. Place the flour in a mixing bowl. Create a well in the middle, and pour in the melted butter and annatto water. Hand mix until the dough is smooth. Cover the bowl with plastic wrap and set aside for 20 minutes to rest.
2. Meanwhile, heat a tablespoon of oil in a pan over medium heat.
3. Sauté the garlic and onion until fragrant.
4. Add the longganisa and stir until the meat is cooked through.
5. Stir in the papaya and season with salt and pepper. Cook for 2 minutes more and set aside to cool.
6. When the dough is ready, divide into six balls.
7. Roll the dough and flatten to form a circle.
8. Scoop about 3 tablespoons of filling onto the center of the dough, crack an egg on top of it, and fold and seal to create a crescent shape.
9. Heat remaining oil in a skillet. Fry empanada until brown and crisp.

(28) Laing

Bicol, located in Southern Luzon (the biggest of the three main islands in the country) has one of the most intricate regional cuisines. With the abundant supply of coconut and chilies, their recipes are mostly characterized by creamy and spicy tastes. Laing is one of the favorite regional cuisines that spread throughout the nation. It features taro leaves (dried or fresh) cooked in a creamy stew, seasoned with chilies, shrimp paste, and pork chunks.

Yield: 8

Cooking Time: 1 hour 20 minutes

List of Ingredients:

- 1-3.5oz pack dried taro leaves
- ½ lb. pork shoulder, thinly sliced
- ½ cup shrimp paste
- ½ cup ginger, sliced
- 8 garlic cloves, crushed
- 1 pc onion, sliced
- 7 pcs red chilies, chopped or left whole
- 6 cups coconut milk
- 2 cups coconut cream

MMMMMMMMMMMMMMMMMMMMMMMMMMMMMMMM

Methods:

1. Combine all of the ingredients in a pot, except for the taro leaves, chilies, and coconut cream. Boil and simmer for 20 minutes.
2. Add the taro leaves and continue cooking for 30 minutes or until the leaves absorb the liquid without stirring.
3. Stir and add the coconut cream and chilies. Stir occasionally until cooked through and creamy.
4. Serve hot.

(29) Caldereta

A good quality beef that was tenderized to perfection is the key to the most delicious *Caldereta*. This dish is a cross between Spanish and Chinese influences. It is seasoned with tomato sauce and tomato sauce, which are products from the foreign countries respectively. It's a favorite for special dinners and all-Filipino party buffets and it well deserves a spot in this cookbook.

Yield: 4

Cooking Time: 2 hours 30 minutes

List of Ingredients:

- 2 lbs. beef, cut into cubes
- 2 pcs potatoes, cubed
- 2 pcs carrots, cubed
- 4 pcs bell pepper, cubed
- 1 cup whole button mushrooms
- 1 cup pineapple tidbits
- 2 garlic cloves, minced
- 1 pc onion, diced
- 1 L tomato sauce
- ½ cup soy sauce
- 1 cup cheese, grated
- 2 cups water
- 1 teaspoon salt
- 1 tablespoon pepper
- 3 Tablespoons olive oil

MMMMMMMMMMMMMMMMMMMMMMMMMMMMMMMMMM

Methods:

1. Heat the oil in a large pan over medium heat.
2. Sauté the garlic and onions until fragrant.
3. Add the beef cubes and brown for about 2 minutes.
4. Pour the water in, season with salt and pepper, and boil.
5. Reduce heat to low and simmer for 1 to 2 hours or until the meat is tender.
6. Whisk in the pineapple tidbits, carrots, potatoes, mushrooms, soy sauce, and tomato sauce. Continue cooking in a simmer for another 20 minutes.
7. Stir in the bell peppers and cheese, then turn off the heat.
8. Serve.

(30) Relyenong Bangus

At first look, this recipe may seem too complicated for an average cook to handle. But in reality, it is not really that challenging. In fact, once you get used to deboning the milkfish without damaging the skin, everything else will be like a walk in the park. Relyenong Bangus is a signature dish that presents an exciting way to enjoy fish altogether. The fish meat is taken, deboned, and flaked before it is combined with a variety of ingredients that somehow give it an entirely different character. It's worth all the work, effort, and patience one needs to put in aside from his kitchen skills.

Yield: 4

Cooking Time: 1 hour 30 minutes

List of Ingredients:

- 1 pc whole milkfish (approximately 2 lbs.), scaled, cleaned and meat and bones removed
- 2 garlic cloves, minced
- 1 pc onion, finely chopped
- 1 pc carrot, finely chopped
- 1 pc potato, finely chopped
- 1 pc red bell pepper, finely chopped
- ½ cup raisins
- ¼ cup pickles, finely chopped
- ½ cup flour
- Juice of 1 lemon
- 3 Tablespoons soy sauce, divided
- 1 cup water
- 2 pcs eggs, lightly beaten
- 1 cup vegetable oil, divided
- Salt and pepper to taste

MMMMMMMMMMMMMMMMMMMMMMMMMMMMMMMMMM

Methods:

1. Place the hollowed skin, 2 tablespoons of soy sauce, and lemon juice in a bowl. Let it sit in the fridge for at least 30 minutes.
2. Meanwhile, boil the fish flesh, together with all its bones in a pan, for about 5 minutes until cooked through. Season with salt and pepper. Set aside to cool.
3. When fish is cool enough to handle, remove bones and flake finely.
4. Heat a tablespoon of oil in a skillet over medium heat and sauté the garlic and onions.
5. Stir in the carrots, potatoes, bell peppers, fish, raisins, and pickles. Continue mixing to blend while cooking the vegetables until softened.
6. Add the remaining soy sauce and some salt and pepper. Turn off heat. Allow the mixture to cool.
7. Whisk in beaten egg into fish mixture once cooled, then, stuff into the marinated skin.
8. Coat fish in flour, removing any excess before frying stuffed fish in hot oil. Cook gently until browned.
9. Drain on paper towels, then slice and serve.

(31) Filipino Style Barbecue

To say that Filipinos love barbecue is an understatement. There are about a hundred and one barbecue variations in this country and they are served widely from street food stalls to hole in the wall restaurants and even in fine dining shops. This pork barbecue recipe is the most prominent variety although they sometimes use almost the same marinade for pork innards, chicken feet, tofu, and others. This recipe is widely consumed with rice, as an appetizer, or along with a bottle of beer.

Yield: 5

Cooking Time: 30 minutes

List of Ingredients:

- 20-30 pcs bamboo skewers, soaked in water overnight
- 2 lbs. pork shoulder, cut into 1-inch strips
- 6 garlic cloves, minced
- 1 pc onion, chopped
- 1 cup soy sauce
- 1 cup banana catsup
- 1 cup clear soda
- ¼ cup calamansi juice
- 1 teaspoon pepper
- 3 Tablespoons brown sugar

MMMMMMMMMMMMMMMMMMMMMMMMMMMMMMMMMM

Methods:

1. Mix all of the ingredients together in a bowl. Cover with plastic wrap and allow the pork to marinade in the spices and sauce mix for 1 hour or better yet, overnight.

2. When ready, thread the pork pieces onto bamboo skewers. Soaking the skewers in water beforehand to help keep it from burning during the grilling process.

3. Heat up the grill.

4. Grill the barbecue until both sides are done, turning a couple of times over, basting leftover sauce each time.

(32) Lechon

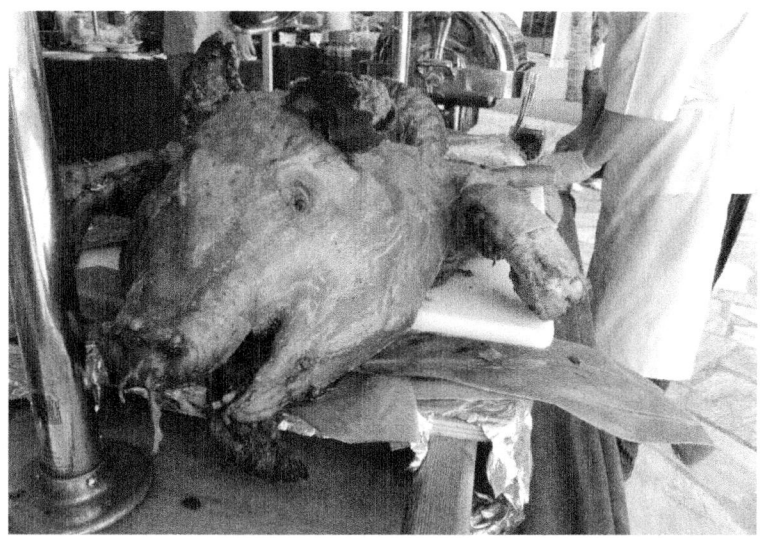

No Filipino feast is complete or is considered grand if a spit-roasted suckling pig is not on the buffet spread. It's a favorite party treat and, sometimes, an everyday meal. There are three different lechon varieties in the Philippines. First is the version of the northern part, in which the pig is seasoned with nothing more than just salt and an agent to make the skin crispy and an appetizing color. Second is the version of the southern Philippines, especially in the Visayas, where lots of elements go inside the pig's stomach, including lemongrass, chorizo de bilbao, and even an entire raw chicken to roast together with the pig (as food guru Anthony

Bourdain's favorite, this is the recipe we are going to follow). Lastly, there's *lechon kawali*, a version that is cooked not in a spit roast but in a deep fryer. Whichever way, lechon is one Filipino recipe in this cookbook that you should not miss, given the fact that it is also a base dish used for other extra-delightful meals like *Lechon Paksiw*, *Sinigang na Lechon*, and many more.

Yield: 12

Cooking Time: 3 hours 5 minutes

List of Ingredients:

- 1 suckling pig (approximately 18 lbs.), cleaned and rinsed
- 2 bunches lemongrass, tied in a knot
- 10 cloves garlic, crushed
- 4 bulbs garlic, cut in half crosswise
- 2 cups onions, peeled and halved
- 2 cups carrots, roughly chopped
- 3 cups light soy sauce
- 3 cups olive oil
- 1 tablespoon salt
- 1 tablespoon pepper, cracked

Methods:

1. Light up the spit roast. It must be extremely hot, white in color, when you start roasting. Before placing the pig, make sure that the coals are moved to the edges. A good bulk should be where the legs and shoulders are. Only a little amount of burning coal must be placed where the midsection of the pig is.

2. Massage the salt, pepper, and crushed garlic onto the cavity of the pig, from the inside and out.

3. Distribute the garlic bulbs, onions, carrots, and lemongrass into the cavity.

4. Pour the soy sauce onto the skin to help you achieve the nice golden brown, deep red color.

5. Secure the midsection by stitching with a heavy wire, making sure the stuffing won't fall off.

6. Carefully insert the axle onto the pig, keeping it in place.

7. Roast the pig for about two hours or until cooked through, constantly moving the pig over and basting the skin with an ample amount of olive oil.

8. Serve hot and carve.

(33) Chicken Galantina

One of the many dishes that make Filipino feasts colorful is this French-inspired dish. 'Galantina' has a direct translation of 'deboning stuffed meat' and that's exactly what this recipe is about. Although traditionally not their very own, Filipinos were able to tweak the dish to add their signature to it.

Yield: 8

Cooking Time: 1 hour 30 minutes

List of Ingredients:

- 3 lbs. whole chicken, deboned
- 1 ½ lbs. ground pork
- 2 pcs ham, finely chopped
- 2 pcs hard-boiled eggs, peeled
- 2 pcs carrots, peeled and boiled
- 1 ½ cup fresh breadcrumbs
- ¼ cup grated cheese
- 1 teaspoon salt
- ½ teaspoons ground white pepper

MMMMMMMMMMMMMMMMMMMMMMMMMMMMMMM

Methods:

1. Preheat oven to 360 °F.
2. Rub the chicken with salt and pepper from inside and out.
3. Mix all of the stuffing ingredients together except for the hard-boiled eggs and carrots.
4. Use half of the mixture to stuff the chicken cavity. Press the boiled carrots and whole hard-boiled eggs inside, then cover with the remaining stuffing.
5. Place the stuffed chicken in a lightly greased baking pan, cover the pan with aluminum foil and bake for one hour.
6. Remove the foil and bake for another 10 minutes until the skin is brown and crisp.
7. Let the chicken rest, then carefully slice before serving.

(34) Papaitan

Speaking of exotic delicacies, here is one recipe that features not just innards but is also interestingly flavored with a bit of bitterness, usually taken from the bile of a cow or goat, based on whichever meat is used. Most definitely, one would have to develop an acquired taste for this soup recipe. If you will concentrate on the taste alone, not minding the other components, there is no reason not to love the dish.

Yield: 8

Cooking Time: 55 minutes

List of Ingredients:

- ½ lb. ox tripe, boiled, rinsed, and sliced
- ½ lb. cow's heart, boiled, rinsed, and sliced
- ½ lb. cow's small intestine, boiled, rinsed, and sliced
- ½ lb. beef, thinly sliced
- 2 Tablespoons bile
- 6 garlic cloves, crushed
- 1 pc onion, diced
- 2 Tablespoons ginger, julienned
- 4 pcs finger chilies
- Juice of 8 pcs calamansi
- 4 cups water
- 2 Tablespoons vegetable oil
- 2 ½ Tablespoons salt
- ½ Tablespoons ground black pepper

MMMMMMMMMMMMMMMMMMMMMMMMMMMMMMMMM

Methods:

1. Heat oil in a pan over medium heat.
2. Sauté the garlic, onion, and ginger, stirring frequently for at least 2 minutes or until fragrant.
3. Add the beef, sliced heart, intestines, and tripe. Cook for about 5 minutes.
4. Season with salt and pepper, then stir to blend.
5. Pour in the water and boil. Reduce heat to low and cook the mixture in a simmer until meats are very tender, about 40 minutes.
6. Stir in the bile and continue to simmer for another 5 minutes.
7. Finally, add the finger chilies and calamansi juice.
8. Serve hot.

(35) Pancit Guisado

This is one of the most Chinese dishes in the Philippines. Pancit pertains to noodles and in the Philippines, as it is in China, there are about a hundred and one varieties of noodles. The most commonly used for the noodle stir-fry might be the regular rice sticks noodles or *bihon* but egg noodles of all sizes, vermicelli, and a combination of the varieties available may also be used. That said, there are also about a hundred and one ways they do the noodle stir-fry, from the most basic type with vegetables and shrimps to the most complex, which may come with intricately concocted sauces and ingredients.

Yield: 4

Cooking Time: 35 minutes

List of Ingredients:

- 1/2 lb. rice sticks noodles, soaked in water for 30 minutes
- ½ lb. pork, sliced
- 5 pcs shrimps, shelled with tails intact
- 1 pc carrot, julienned
- 1 cup cabbage, cut into strips
- 1 pc red bell pepper, seeded and julienned
- 2 garlic cloves, minced
- 1 pc onion, sliced
- ½ cup soy sauce
- 1 teaspoon fish sauce
- 2 cups chicken broth
- 1 tablespoon cooking oil
- Salt and pepper to taste
- 4 pcs calamansi, halved, for garnish

MMMMMMMMMMMMMMMMMMMMMMMMMMMMMMMMMM

Methods:

1. Drain the noodles and rinse. Set aside.
2. Heat the oil in a wok over medium heat and sauté the garlic and onions.
3. Add pork slices and cook for 3-5 minutes until they change in color.
4. Put in the shrimp and continue stirring for about a minute or two.
5. Add the carrots and bell peppers.
6. Whisk in the soy sauce and fish sauce, plus the broth. Mix to blend and boil.
7. Add the noodles, stirring frequently for about 10 minutes, so the noodles separate and cooked through while blending with the rest of the ingredients.
8. Season the noodles with salt and pepper. You may also add more broth if it starts to dry, then stir in cabbage.
9. Remove from heat and serve with calamansi.

About the Author

A native of Indianapolis, Indiana, Valeria Ray found her passion for cooking while she was studying English Literature at Oakland City University. She decided to try a cooking course with her friends and the experience changed her forever. She enrolled at the Art Institute of Indiana which offered extensive courses in the culinary Arts. Once Ray dipped her toe in the cooking world, she never looked back.

When Valeria graduated, she worked in French restaurants in the Indianapolis area until she became the head chef at one of the 5-star establishments in the area. Valeria's attention to taste and visual detail caught the eye of a local business person who expressed an interest in publishing her recipes. Valeria began her secondary career authoring cookbooks and e-books which she tackled with as much talent and gusto as her first career. Her passion for food leaps off the page of her books which have colourful anecdotes and stunning pictures of dishes she has prepared herself.

Valeria Ray lives in Indianapolis with her husband of 15 years, Tom, her daughter, Isobel and their loveable Golden Retriever, Goldy. Valeria enjoys cooking special dishes in her large, comfortable kitchen where the family gets involved in preparing meals. This successful, dynamic chef is an inspiration to culinary students and novice cooks everywhere.

•••••••••••••••••••••••

Author's Afterthoughts

Thank you for Purchasing my book and taking the time to read it from front to back. I am always grateful when a reader chooses my work and I hope you enjoyed it!

With the vast selection available online, I am touched that you chose to be purchasing my work and take valuable time out of your life to read it. My hope is that you feel you made the right decision.

I very much would like to know what you thought of the book. Please take the time to write an honest and informative review on Amazon.com. Your experience and opinions will be of great benefit to me and those readers looking to make an informed choice.

With much thanks,

Valeria Ray

Printed in Great Britain
by Amazon

15576608R00068